# IMAGES OF WAR
# THE WAFFEN-SS ON THE EASTERN FRONT

## RARE PHOTOGRAPHS FROM WARTIME ARCHIVES

# IMAGES OF WAR

# THE WAFFEN-SS ON THE EASTERN FRONT

## RARE PHOTOGRAPHS FROM WARTIME ARCHIVES

## BOB CARRUTHERS

Pen & Sword
**MILITARY**

This edition published in 2015 by

Pen & Sword Military
An imprint of
Pen & Sword Books Ltd.
47 Church Street
Barnsley
South Yorkshire
S70 2AS

ISBN: 9781783462452

A CIP catalogue record for this book is available from the British Library.

Printed and bound in England
By CPI Group (UK) Ltd., Croydon, CR0 4YY

Pen & Sword Books Ltd. incorporates the imprints of Pen & Sword Aviation, Pen & Sword Family History, Pen & Sword Maritime, Pen & Sword Military, Pen & Sword Discovery, Pen & Sword Politics, Pen & Sword Atlas, Pen & Sword Archaeology, Wharncliffe Local History, Wharncliffe True Crime, Wharncliffe Transport, Pen & Sword Select, Pen & Sword Military Classics, Leo Cooper, The Praetorian Press, Claymore Press, Remember When, Seaforth Publishing and Frontline Publishing

For a complete list of Pen & Sword titles please contact

PEN & SWORD BOOKS LIMITED
47 Church Street, Barnsley, South Yorkshire, S70 2AS, England
E-mail: enquiries@pen-and-sword.co.uk
Website: www.pen-and-sword.co.uk

# INTRODUCTION

Based on the evidence of their combat record the Waffen-SS are often hailed as an elite fighting force. However, while it is true that this force fought exceptionally well in military terms, in social and humanitarian terms the reputation of the Waffen-SS, the armed political wing which grew out of the *Schutzstaffel* or Nazi party protection squads, will always be tainted by the war crimes they committed in the East and West. Their litany of crimes in the Soviet Union included the killing of those the Nazis designated as *untermenschen* or sub humans – Slavs, Jews and Marxists.

The Waffen-SS was one of the weapons in the Nazi arsenal which was used to wage the unlooked for war which was to lead its architects to the courtroom at Nuremberg. These men you see here were the Nazi idealists who had bought into the Nazi creed of expansion to the east in search of *Lebensraum*.

The *Lebensraum* ideology proposed an aggressive expansion of Germany and the German people. The Nazis supported territorial expansionism to gain *Lebensraum* as being a law of nature. The Nazi creed espoused the idea that it was necessary for all healthy and vigorous peoples of superior races to displace people of inferior races; especially if the people of a superior race were facing overpopulation in their given territories. The hierarchy of the Nazi Party believed that Germany inevitably needed to territorially expand because it was indeed facing an overpopulation crisis which Adolf Hitler described as follows: "We are overpopulated and cannot feed ourselves from our own resources." It was on this basis that expansion eastwards was justified as an inevitable necessity for Germany. From 1939 to 1941, the Nazi regime gave the outward appearance of having discarded plans to annex Soviet territories, this deceptive stance was strengthened by the improved relations with the Soviet Union via the Molotov-Ribbentrop Pact, and the public claims that central Africa was where Germany sought to achieve *Lebensraum*. Hitler publicly claimed that Germany wanted to settle the *Lebensraum* issue peacefully through diplomatic negotiations that would require other powers to make concessions to Germany; at the same time however Germany prepared for war in the cause of *Lebensraum*, and the potential clash between the peoples of Germany and the Soviet Union.

In 1941, it was the stated policy of the Nazis to kill, deport, or enslave the Polish, Ukrainian, Russian, and other Slavic populations, whom they considered inferior, and to repopulate the land with Germanic people drawn primarily from the ranks of the Waffen-SS. The urban population was considered disposable and could potentially be exterminated by starvation, thus creating an agricultural surplus to feed Germany and allowing their replacement by the population of warrior farmers who were to be rewarded with grants of land in recognition for their service in the ranks of the Waffen-SS. The policy of *Lebensraum* implicitly assumed the superiority of Germans as members of an Aryan master race who by virtue of their superiority had the right to displace people deemed to be part of inferior races. The Nazis insisted that *Lebensraum* needed to be developed as racially homogeneous to avoid intermixing with peoples deemed to be part of inferior races, with its strict entry requirements the Waffen-SS was the prime instrument in Hitler's vision The man who was to give concrete form was Heinrich Himmler and it was he who was the real driving force behind the Waffen-SS in practical terms. The vague rhetoric spouted by Hitler had to be translated into practicality by Himmler. Hitler, as always had no concrete plan, as a result, those peoples deemed to be inferior races living within territory selected for *Lebensraum* were subject to arbitrary expulsion, enslavement or destruction.

Hitler gave a speech to his Waffen-SS troops just three weeks before the start of Operation Barbarossa, the Nazi code name for the attack on the Soviet Union. He said, "This is an ideological battle and a struggle of races. Here stands a world as we conceived it – beautiful, decent, socially equal and full of culture; this is what our Germany is like. On the other side stands a population of 180,000,000, a mixture of races, whose very names are unpronounceable and whose physique is such that one can only shoot them down without mercy or compassion. When you fight over there in the east, you are carrying on the same struggle against the same sub-humanity, the same inferior races, that at one time appeared under the name of Huns, another time of Magyars, another time of Tartars, and still another time under the name of Genghis Khan and the Mongols. Today they appear as Russians under the political banner of Bolshevism."

When he launched operation Barbarossa Hitler expected the *Wehrmacht* (the German armed forces) to conquer the Soviet Union and the Waffen-SS to carry out the goals of the party. To the *Wehrmacht* Hitler ordered the job of "kicking in the front door so the whole rotten Russian edifice will come tumbling down". To the Waffen-SS therefore fell not just the job of combat but also waging a race war to create Hitler's long cherished dream of *Lebensraum*, the much-anticipated living space for the German people in the East. However, as events spiralled out of control, the war in the east became the most titanic struggle in the history of human conflict. From the opening moves the scale of the struggle was truly colossal. On one side were over three million well trained, equipped and battle hardened German troops including the Waffen-SS and half a million of their Axis allies. In total the Germans deployed 153 divisions including 21 Panzer and 14 motorised divisions containing over 3,400 tanks and 3000 aircraft. On the other side was a Soviet army of over five million men in 180 divisions with over 10,000 tanks and 20,000 aircraft.

This was a genuine life or death struggle, during operations in the East the Waffen-SS grew from just six divisions comprising 160,000 men at the start of Barbarossa until, by the end of the war, it represented a huge force of 38 combat divisions comprising over 950,000 men. Under the command of Heinrich Himmler, the Waffen-SS received privileged treatment in terms of weapons and supplies. As a consequence they attracted only the most committed recruits who were willing to fight and die for the cause. Not surprisingly with their advantages which sprang from highly motivated recruits, excellent equipment, cohesive background requirements and an all-embracing ideological indoctrination, the Waffen-SS soon earned a fearsome reputation in combat.

Heinrich Himmler

In the East Waffen-SS divisions were placed under the operational control of the *Oberkommando des Heeres* or the Supreme High Command of the Army although in practice they often acted independently. Initially the Waffen-SS was numerically insignificant when compared to regular Germany Army, however the Waffen-SS brought to Barbarossa an ideological fanaticism out of all proportion to their numbers. This sense of racial and military superiority, which was encouraged by Himmler and maintained through better pay, food and equipment, was central to the Waffen-SS philosophy. It was combined with a fanatical loyalty to Hitler, and encapsulated in the motto *"Meine Ehre heißt Treue"* or "My honour is loyalty". It meant that at the start of Barbarossa five of the six divisions which comprised the Waffen-SS in the field (the *Leibstandarte Adolf Hitler*, *Das Reich*, *Totenkopf*, *Polizei* and *Nord*) were all recruited from the toughest and most ideological ethnic Germans. The exception was the *Wiking* division, which was recruited from ideologically motivated Scandinavian, Finish, Estonian, Dutch and Belgian volunteers, but served under German officers.

German society had been indoctrinated with a sense of obedience and orders were to be followed without question. The men of the regular army had no qualms when it came to following orders; however distasteful. However, for the over-stretched regular German Army activities like racial cleansing, which did not progress their war aims, was regarded with disdain but characterised as a waste of resources rather than as a crime. From the Waffen-SS viewpoint this attitude was incomprehensible; to the men of the Waffen-SS the regular army lacked the ideology necessary to secure the final victory. The result was a severely strained relationship between the two who often disagreed on all aspects of how the campaign should be fought from the tactical to the strategic level.

The *Wehrmacht* launched its surprise attack on Russia at 3.15am on 22 June 1941, bombing positions in Soviet occupied Poland. Attached to the three huge army groups were the six Waffen-SS divisions. Army Group North advanced through the Baltic States and on to Leningrad, included in its ranks were *Totenkopf*, *Polizei* and *Nord*. Army Group Centre headed towards Moscow with *Das Reich* in the vanguard. *Leibstandarte* and *Wiking* were with Army Group South and marched towards the Ukraine and Kiev.

During the first six months of Barbarossa the sheer scale of the Soviet rout in the East surprised even the German generals. On the opening day alone the *Luftwaffe* destroyed over 2000 Soviet aircraft, many on the ground and Army Group North penetrated over 50 miles into Russian territory. By the end of the first week Army Group Centre had captured Minsk and by the end of June they had advanced over 200 miles towards Moscow. By the end of September Army Group South had captured nearly half a million Soviet troops during the Battle of Kiev and Army Group North had lay siege to Leningrad. At the spearhead of all these successful advances in the East were the men of the Waffen-SS.

Yet just three months later the offensive ground to a shuddering halt. On 1 December 1941, in temperatures of minus 40 Fahrenheit, the offensive stalled at the tram terminus on the very outskirts of Moscow. Five days later the Red Army counterattacked driving the Germans back 40 miles. During Operation Typhoon or the attack on Moscow *Das Reich* suffered catastrophic losses and of the 2000 men who had started out with the regiment in June 1941, only 35 were left alive by the end of December. While the defeat was a crushing defeat for Germany it was to prove, in some respects at least, the making of the Waffen-SS.

By the end of 1941 the Waffen-SS had suffered over 43,000 casualties across the length of the Eastern Front. One in four Waffen-SS troops had either been killed or wounded. However, it was widely recognised, even by the *Wehrmacht*, that they had fought with great tenacity and without them the German army would not have got to the gates of Moscow. Eberhard von Macksensen, commander of III Army Corps in Army Group South, writing to Himmler said the *Leibstandarte* had demonstrated "inner discipline, cool daredevilry, cheerful enterprise, unshakeable firmness in a crisis, exemplary toughness and camaraderie". The legend of the fanatical fighting spirit of the Waffen-SS had been born.

By the beginning of 1942, the Soviet Union was bloodied but unbowed. The changing fortunes of the campaign were reflected by the encirclement of 100,000 Germans troops from Army Group North who, in February 1942, were trapped in the Demyansk pocket south of Leningrad. The pocket included the SS Division *Totenkopf* who again were at the forefront of the fighting and who eventually led the breakout in April 1942. However, they paid a high price with 15,000 troops either killed or wounded. After this the Waffen-SS were never again to regain the initiative in the East but they were to fight with distinction at Kharkov and Kursk.

From 1943 to 1945, the Waffen-SS, in the East were engaged in a long and bloody retreat against a numerically far superior enemy. As they fell back across the vast plains of the Soviet Union, Poland, Hungary and ultimately Germany itself, all too often their fate became death or ignominious defeat at the hands of the Red Army. But the Waffen-SS, true to their character, fought a fanatical rearguard action to the end. In the process they demonstrated, what were, by objective standards, heroic, if increasingly futile, acts of bravery against overwhelming odds.

The tipping point in the East was the Soviet Union's vastly superior forces in terms of men, planes, and crucially armour, which, after 1942, began to decisively alter the outcome of the war. In order to counter the threat of the formidable Soviet T-34 the Germans had developed new tanks such as the Panther and the Tiger, but they simply could not produce them in sufficient quantities to make a difference. By the end of the war the Germans had produced nearly 6,000 Panthers and just over 1,300 Tiger tanks. In comparison the Russians were building over 1,200 T-34 tanks each month.

The devastating defeat at Stalingrad in February 1943 epitomised the changing fortunes of the *Wehrmacht* in the East. To counter what he interpreted as the defeatist attitude of the army, Hitler increasingly turned to the Waffen-SS whose loyalty and fighting spirit were never in question. The *Wehrmacht's* loss became the Waffen-SS's gain as the *Führer's* "fire brigade" were used to plug the gaps and hold the line against the marauding Red Army.

By 1945, under the operational command of Heinrich Himmler, Hitler had created 38 Waffen-SS divisions and had resorted to conscripting over 900,000 men. As the situation in the East deteriorated they were drawn from an ever more diverse ethnic mix typified by the 13th Waffen-SS *Handschar* Division which was composed of Bosnian Muslims. This unit conducted anti-partisan activities in Yugoslavia and Croatia during 1944. The result was that by the finish of the Second World War nearly half of the Waffen-SS were non-ethnic Germans despite the original strict racial requirements laid down by Himmler.

To the end Hitler possessed an almost blind faith in the fighting ability of the Waffen-SS. This was despite the fact that many of the later divisions were only regiment or brigade sized units. Furthermore the ranks were all too often filled by conscripts who lacked the experience, élan and *esprit de corps* of the original formations. As losses mounted the cadres from the original elite SS divisions were amalgamated to form mechanised Panzer Corps, these formations soon became the backbone of the German Army.

In March 1943, Hitler's faith in the SS Panzer Corps was rewarded. Under the charismatic leadership of Paul "Papa" Hausser, nicknamed the father of the Waffen-SS, they pulled off a spectacular victory at Kharkov, the second largest city in the Ukraine, temporarily halting the Soviet advance. The pictures in this book bear witness to the dash they showed in the face of an overwhelming enemy.

Hausser's Panzer Corps had found themselves trapped in the city and with the defeat at Stalingrad still a fresh memory Hitler ordered them to "stand fast and fight to the death". Risking Hitler's wrath Hausser ignored his direct orders and instead sanctioned a strategic withdraw to prevent his tanks being decimated in the besieged city. In response Hitler flew into a blind rage and tried to sack his wayward commander. However, Hausser regrouped and without *Luftwaffe* support made a direct attack on Kharkov, eventually recapturing the city after four days of intensive, house-to-house fighting. For his bravery Hausser was awarded the Oak Leaves to his Knights Cross and officially pardoned.

Others honoured with the Knights Cross, the highest award for bravery given by Nazi Germany, included Joachim Peiper, a reconnaissance commander who developed a tactic of attacking enemy-held villages by night from all sides while advancing in his armoured half-tracks at full speed, firing at every building. This tactic often set the building's straw roofs on fire and contributed to panic among enemy troops. As a result Peiper's unit gained the nickname the "Blowtorch Battalion".

Paul "Papa" Hausser

The Battle of Kharkov was the third time the city had changed sides since the start of Operation Barbarossa, it was also to be the last victory for the Waffen-SS in the East. The offensive resulted in the Red Army suffering over 70,000 casualties, but in an ominous sign of the battles to come the SS Panzer Corps lost nearly half its combat strength.

Ironically the success of the Third Battle of Kharkov was to prove a turning point in the East not for Hitler but for Stalin because it lulled the Germans back into a false sense of their own superiority. Reinvigorated by the victory, in July 1943, Hitler sought to eliminate the Kursk salient, a bulge where the Soviet advance jutted westwards for about 80 miles into the German line. The result was Operation Citadel, the largest tank battle in history. It pitched 900,000 Germans with 2,700 tanks and 2,000 aircraft against some 1.3 million Russians with 3,600 tanks and 2,400 aircraft. Once again the Waffen-SS were in the forefront of the fighting.

The German plan was to cut off the Kursk salient by making two pincer attacks at its neck. However, unknown to the Germans the Soviets had received prior intelligence about the attack from the so called "Lucy" spy ring based in Switzerland, acting on information provided by special operations at Bletchley Park in Oxfordshire. Stalin's commanders had therefore persuaded him to allow the Germans to attack and instead fall back to well-prepared defensive positions before counterattacking. The Waffen-SS fell into the carefully laid trap.

On 5 July 1943, the northern offensive was launched and spearheaded by the SS Panzer Corps. With characteristic determination they took the attack to the enemy, and penetrated deep into the Soviet territory. When the advance eventually slowed after 22 miles of savage fighting, the Germans had destroyed over 1,149 tanks, 459 anti-tank guns, 85 aircraft and 47 artillery pieces. However, the Russians fell back on impenetrable defensive positions composed of vast minefields, innumerable field guns and supporting armour. The German offensive soon stalled and the 1st Soviet Army counterattacked inflicting large casualties on the SS Panzer Corps, forcing them into headlong retreat. The issue was decided when, a week later, six US and British divisions landed in Sicily. Fearing an imminent invasion of Italy Hitler diverted the remaining two SS Panzer Corps two thousand kilometres to the west.

The remains of the Waffen-SS in the East now found themselves constantly on the retreat. On 25 August Kharkov once again fell to the Soviets, this time for good. By the beginning of September the Germans had suffered over half a million casualties in fifty days and 1,600 tanks and assault guns had been destroyed or knocked out. Soviet casualties are not known but historians estimate the total to be twice the number of

German losses. Nonetheless, for Hitler the losses were unsustainable and the Battle of Kursk proved to be the last German offensive in the East. Alexander Kovalenko, a Soviet pilot, flying over a battlefield littered with German armour declared triumphantly "The enemy's front is broken. We are advancing."

Joachim Peiper

After Kursk morale in the army began to disintegrate but in the Waffen-SS a fanatical, if increasingly futile, fighting spirit lived on. Panzer Officer Tassilo von Bogenhardt was typical and said after the battle "Each German soldier considered himself superior to any single Russian, even though their numbers were so overpowering. The slow, orderly retreat did not depress us too much. We felt we were holding our own." His illusion was rudely shattered shortly afterwards when he was badly wounded and then captured by the Soviets, the worst fate that could befall a Waffen-SS soldier.

By the end of 1943, half the territory taken by the Germans since 1941, was back under Soviet control. Russia had lost over twenty million men but they were no longer on their own. The Allies had successfully invaded Italy and, six months late, on 6 June 1944, came the D-Day landings. For the Waffen-SS this meant fighting on two fronts and more divisions being diverted from the East to the West, further weakening their ability to defend the "Fatherland against Bolshevism".

Even in retreat, however, the Waffen-SS proved themselves to be a formidable fighting unit. Typical of this trend was Herbert Gille, commander of the 5th SS-Panzer Division *Wiking*. In an almost suicidal move he broke out of the Korsun-Cherkassy Pocket in Northern Ukraine in 1944, against overwhelming Russian odds. For his bravery he received the Diamonds to add to his Knight Cross. Also worthy of note is *Obertsturmbannführer* or Lieutenant Colonel Leon Degrelle, commander of the 28th Waffen-SS Division *Walloon* from Belgium. During the retreat of his division to the border of Germany in 1944, he was severely wounded but carried on fighting. As a result he was one of only three foreigners to win the Oak Leaves to the Knights Cross. He received it from Hitler's hands and later claimed Hitler told him "If I had a son, I wish he'd resemble you."

On May Day 1944, Stalin declared "If we are to deliver our country and those of our allies from the danger of enslavement, we must pursue the wounded German beast and deliver the final blow to him in his own lair." The Soviets started their pursuit on 22 June 1944, when they launched Operation Bagration, the largest and most successful offensive to be launched from Russian soil. This left the remaining Waffen-SS divisions defending a 1,000 mile front with few reserves. It was the beginning of the end.

As the war in the East moved to Poland and eventually Germany, Waffen-SS troops were among the final soldiers defending the ruins of the Reich Chancellery in Berlin.

Dr. Oskar Paul Dirlewanger

Hitler finally committed suicide on 30 April 1945, and when news of his death reached them, many of the remaining Waffen-SS troops shot themselves rather than surrender to the Soviets.

After hostilities had finally ceased on 8 May 1945, nearly one in three Waffen-SS troops were dead or missing in action. For an elite fighting force which never made up more than 10% of the total German Army and had numbered just 120 men in 1933, they had fought with almost reckless courage and paid a very high price. Their mortality rate was the equivalent of all the casualties suffered by the United States military during the entire war.

The Waffen-SS had been overwhelmed by an enemy simply too strong in men and material. However, as their military situation had worsened so had their atrocities; while some non-combatant units were most obviously culpable for much of the ethnic cleansing operations, no member of the civil population could consider themselves safe from these armed ideologists. Praise for the Waffen-SS as an elite fighting force in the annals of the Second World War therefore needs to be balanced against their sinister motive and the utter ruthlessness they showed, particularly towards the Jews, Soviets and later the Poles in the suppression of the Warsaw uprising in 1944. It was here that Dr. Oskar Paul Dirlewanger commanded the infamous Waffen-SS penal unit *Dirlewanger*. Dirlewanger was not alone and although his name is most closely linked to some of the worst crimes of the war, we can be certain that a host of similar crimes have gone unreported. Accordingly history has judged the Waffen-SS not as they would have wished – by their combat record – but instead far more ignominiously by the atrocities they carried out. When historians review the campaign in the East the fighting record of the Waffen-SS is rightly seen in the context of Hitler's ideological war against the Soviet Union. As a result there is an indelible stain on their combat record and after the war many Waffen-SS veterans were deprived of pension rights. While it is an indisputable fact that the Waffen-SS were involved in atrocities and war crimes, at the individual level there were those who fought honourably amidst the fog of war which afflicted both sides.

War crimes aside, as these pictures demonstrate, many Waffen-SS troops distinguished themselves in combat and showed incredible bravery, often against overwhelming odds. The military esteem with which the Waffen-SS were regarded can perhaps best be judged, not by their rivals in the *Wehrmacht*, but by their hated adversaries in the Red Army. At the victory parade in Red Square in Moscow on 24 June 1945, pride of place among the captured Nazi standards was reserved for the banner of first Waffen-SS division, the *Leibstandarte Adolf Hitler*.

Operation Barbarossa was the German codename for the attack on Russia. The attack commenced at 3.15 a.m. on 22 June 1941. Over 3 million German troops and half a million of its allies attacked across an 1,800 mile front in three massive army groups. The *Wehrmacht* was accompanied by six Waffen-SS Divisions.

Army Group North advanced through the Baltic States and on to Leningrad, it contained three Waffen-SS Divisions; *Totenkopf*, *Polizei* and *Nord*. Army Group Centre headed to Moscow with *Das Reich*. *Leibstandarte* and *Wiking* were with Army Group South and drove towards Ukraine and Kiev.

Motorcycles of the *Wiking* Division scout ahead of the Panzers. The speed and ferocity of the German attack caught the Russians completely by surprise.

Huge demands were made on the infantry who had to march vast distances of up to 40 miles a day in order to keep up with the fast moving Panzers.

A thorough search of every building had to be undertaken.

The wing of a crashed Soviet aircraft makes a sign-post for the troops following in the wake of the rapidly advancing reconnaissance section.

Russian prisoners are interrogated in order to gain valuable information on enemy dispositions.

Russian prisoners await evacuation from the battlefield. These men faced the prospect of inhuman treatment which saw millions die from disease and maltreatment.

The dismal sight of the displaced civilian population caught up in the fighting was an omnipresent and depressing sight for the men of the Waffen-SS.

*Totenkopf* troops leave behind a burning Russian village in the opening weeks of Barbarossa. The division was notorious for its ethnic cleansing. The Death's Head insignia reflected the fact that many early recruits were concentration camp guards.

A close up of a *Totenkopf* motorcycle. Note the swastika on the side car, used for recognition by the *Luftwaffe*.

A 20mm Flak 30 anti-aircraft gun is brought up to support the attack. Although designed as an anti-aircraft gun it was also extensively used as an infantry support gun. It was the most numerous German artillery gun produced during the war.

Waffen-SS grenadiers take cover behind the shield of a 7.5cm le.IG 18 infantry support gun.

The 6th Panzer Division *Das Nord* fought with Army Group North and saw action right up to the Arctic Circle. Here they have brought up a 7.5cm leichtes Infanteriegeschütz 18 or 7.5cm le.IG 18 infantry support gun to fire on partisans hiding in the woods and marshes of Karelia.

A Waffen-SS *Leinstandarte* BMW R75 motorcyclist and his outrider watch as buildings burn. The German army insisted that both BMW and their rivals Zündapp use almost 70% of the same motorcycle components to simplify the supply of spares.

Waffen-SS *Funker* or radio operator receives a message for his unit. The attack on Russia posed a serious challenge in terms of communication because of the speed of the advance and the great distances involved along the fronts.

Waffen-SS troops firing an MG 42 machine gun. It was the standard machine gun from 1942 onwards replacing the MG 34, and had one of the highest rates of fire of any single barrelled gun at 1,200–1,500 rounds per minute.

Waffen-SS troops using an anti-tank gun against the Soviet T-34 tank. The T-34 was heavily armoured and it required a direct hit to its tracks or at very close range to disable it.

Sepp Dietrich, commander *Leibstandarte*, watches over the advance of his troops. He was to end the war as one of Nazi Germany's most decorated commanders.

*Das Reich* troops in a Russian village during the opening weeks of the campaign, June 1941. They were attached to Army Group Centre whose objective was to take Moscow. Note the *Wolfsangel* or Wolf's Hook insignia on the front right wheel arch, the symbol for *Das Reich*.

*Totenkopf* troops crossing a makeshift bridge in a Horsh 108 troop carrier. Note the Death's Head insignia on the rear.

The reconnaissance battlion of the SS *Wiking* Division scout ahead of the infantry and tanks. *Wiking* Division was recruited from Scandinavian, Finish, Estonian, Dutch and Belgian volunteers but served under German officers. However, recruitment proved to be sluggish and the bulk of the rank and file were German citizens.

*Totenkopf* troops rest in a copse during a lull in the fighting, September 1941. They were attached to Army Group North who advanced through the Baltic States and on to Leningrad.

A Waffen-SS soldier from *Leibstandarte* Division watches a village burn. As the campaign progressed many Soviet fighters, rather than surrender went into hiding and formed partisan units who operated behind German lines.

*Sturmgeschutzen* lead the attack against Soviet forces on the outskirts of the port of Mariupol in Ukraine. The city fell on 8 October 1941 giving the Germans access to the Sea of Azov. The attack on Russia would see German and Axis troops attacking in three huge army groups along a vast front which grew longer as they advanced.

Soldiers from the *Wiking* Division use a flamethrower against Soviet troops. This Model 35 flamethrower had a capacity of 2.5 gallons and a range of 25 yards. They were operated by engineers rather than combat troops and were most effective at close range against pillboxes.

Horses and armour both played a pivotal role in Operation Barbarossa. While the Panzer tanks were mechanically complex and prone to breakdown, many horses were simply worked until they dropped from exhaustion, hunger or disease.

German soldiers preparing ammunition for their unit. The sheer speed of the advance during the early months of Barbarossa meant that providing enough ammunition for the troops was a constant logistical challenge.

SS *Totenkopf* officers drive to the front in a Volkswagen Kubelwagen Type 82, the German equivalent of a jeep, 1941. Although more comfortable than a jeep, its low centre of gravity meant it struggled with the deep mud in Russia.

The Russian winter took a very heavy toll on the Germans who unlike the Soviets were not equipped with winter clothing. By November 1941, the Germans had suffered 730,000 casualties.

Waffen-SS troops put together a "Panzer cocktail", an improvised Molotov cocktail used against the Russian T-34 tank. Due to its sloping armour the 3.7cm anti-tank gun proved ineffective against it.

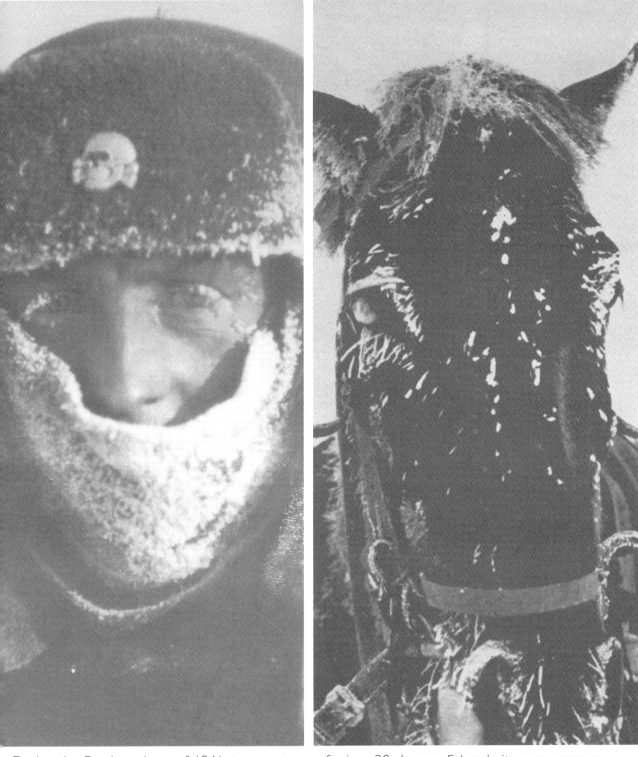

During the Russian winter of 1941, temperatures of minus 20 degrees Fahrenheit were common affecting both men and animals.

An SS Calvary Division patrol during the winter of 1941. The deep snow slowed the German advance in November and played a key role in the halting the German offensive in December.

*Das Reich*, part of Army Group Centre, reached the gates of Moscow in December 1941 but the weather, massive losses and a Soviet counter-offensive forced the division back.

During the Russian winter of 1941 German troops soon became experts at putting up makeshift shelters against the cold.

Waffen-SS sniper on the Eastern Front. He is equipped with the standard German army rifle the Karbiner 98k Kurz with a telescopic sight. Rifles which were exceptionally accurate in factory tests were specifically allocated to snipers for this task. They had an effective range of 1,000 metres.

A German convoy makes slow progress through a snow storm. Conditions demoralised the German troops as did their distance from home. Nearly a thousand miles separated Moscow and Berlin.

From their positions west of Moscow soldiers in *Das Reich* could clearly see the Soviet capital through their binoculars. It was the closest they would ever get. The German army would never again threaten the Russian capital.

Soldiers from *Das Reich* Division rest on the outskirts of Moscow, December 1941. The division was decimated by the Soviet counter-offensive and was withdrawn for rest and refitting.

A Waffen-SS *Oberscharführer* or platoon leader scans the horizon for Soviet troops. The Russian winter gave the Soviets a respite from the German advance and allowed them to plan their counter-offensive.

German troops take cover in a copse and scan the horizon. In the depths of winter woods not only provided cover from the enemy but also from the elements.

A Waffen-SS soldier emerges from his dug out. Over 100,000 German troops suffered from frostbite, the more serious cases requiring amputation.

Russian peasants watch as a German motorcycle and side car rushes past towards the front. As *untermenschen* or sub humans, the Germans treated them with contempt which simply stiffened their resolve to fight.

The 8th SS Calvary Division was named after Florian Geyer, a sixteenth century nobleman who was famous for leading the peasants during the German Peasants War. Mounted infantry regiments were operating as autonomous units with the army during 1942 and 1943.

Waffen-SS engineers build a bridge while others bathe naked in the river. Engineers were attached to every unit and were a vital part of the German war effort, helping to overcome whatever obstacles were placed in the way of the advancing army.

Soviet Partisans use a horn to call for the surrender of trapped German troops. Propaganda was an important tool for both sides during the campaign and the Germans and Russians made extensive use of leaflets dropped behind enemy lines.

Waffen-SS soldiers attached to Army Group South cross the River Pripyat in the Ukraine. They were surrounded by vast marshes which provided many hiding places for Soviet partisans who regularly attacked the German advance.

Outclassed by the Russian T-34 and KV tanks and difficult to repair, the Panzer III was nevertheless the core of the German mechanised divisions and over 5,700 were built.

An SS radio operator receives their next orders. Good communication between the Panzer tanks and the infantry was what made the German war machine so successful.

A Tiger tank commander with the 3rd SS Divison *Totenkopf*. The division suffered heavy casualties during the Battle of the Demjansk Pocket, but went on to fight with distinction at the Battle of Kursk in 1943.

A Waffen-SS unit on operations against Soviet partisans. They were a resistance movement modelled on the Red Army who fought a guerrilla campaign against the Germans rear lines, successfully disrupting road and rail communications. Here an 8cm Granatwerfer 34 mortar is carried through the woods. The barrel, baseplate, stand and shells all had to be carried by hand, making it a three man job to transport the mortar.

A German motorcyclist sunbathes. Motorcyclists were crucial to the German offensive being more mobile and able to cover large distances much more quickly than other motorised vehicles.

A Waffen-SS radio operator climbs on a roof to erect an aerial. Radio and reconnaissance units were particularly targeted by Soviet partisans to disrupt German lines of communication which were already stretched by the vast distances involved in the campaign.

A German soldier guards Russian prisoners. After 1941 the capture of large numbers of Soviet troops became much rarer with many preferring to fight and die rather than surrender.

The 7th SS Volunteer Mountain Division *Prinz Eugen* was formed in March 1942 from ethnic Germans volunteers from Vojvodina, Croatia, Hungary and Romania and was engaged in anti-partisan operations in the Balkans.

A Flak 30 or 20mm anti-aircraft gun in action. A lightweight gun, it was easy to transport but its low fire power of only 120 rounds a minute let it down.

Waffen-SS troops cross a river on the Atlantic coast in August 1942. Waffen-SS divisions were withdrawn from the fierce fighting on the Eastern Front to recuperate and be refitted in the West.

Max Simon, commander of the 1st Regiment of the *Totenkopf* Division, was awarded the Knight's Cross for the fighting in the Battles of the Demyansk Pocket and promoted to *Oberführer* or Brigadier General. In December 1942 Simon was promoted again to *Brigadeführer* or Major General, prior to being given command of the 16th SS *Panzergrenadier* Division *Reichsführer-SS*.

Hellmuth Becker, centre, later commander of the 3rd SS Panzer Division *Totenkopf*, resting in a trench after fierce fighting in the Demyansk pocket. He was awarded the Knights Cross of the Iron Cross for his bravery.

An SS officer talks with *Wehrmacht* commanders during Barbarossa. The Waffen-SS and the *Wehrmacht* had a difficult relationship and often did not agree on strategy, meaning attacks were not always well co-ordinated.

A *Leibstandarte Schwerer Panzerspähwagen* or heavy armoured reconnaissance vehicle patrols the streets of a Russian town. This model was easy to spot because of the heavy "bedstead" antenna over the body of the vehicle used for the short wave radio.

Men of the *Wiking* division just prior to their attack on the vital city of Grozny in September 1942. During the battle the division was to lose over 1,500 men and failed to capture the city. It was to be a turning point in its campaign and the first of many setbacks.

Waffen-SS men relax prior to battle. They wore a wide range of uniforms from the *feldgrau* or field grey similar to the regular army to the mottled camouflage which was their hallmark.

Waffen-SS troops pull a motorcycle through the mud. Unlike in the West, many Russian roads were not surfaced and quickly turned to mud after the rains.

Lorries make their way gingerly through a swollen river after the big thaw following the Soviet winter of 1941/42. The thaw could turn even a ford into a raging torrent.

Waffen-SS troops advance cautiously in an armed vehicle. Soviet troops had learnt from the opening months of the campaign becoming experts at using the terrain to ambush German patrols.

A German Panzer III tank crew rest and watch the units mascot, a German Alsatian dog. German officers were allowed to keep dogs which were not meant to be pets but working dogs designed to boost morale.

The Waffen-SS were quick to utilise captured T-34 tanks ("*Beutepanzer*"), marking them with German insignia. However, this was never a popular assignment as anti-tank crews would often fire on sighting the familiar silhouette of the T-34 at long range.

A curious Waffen-SS grenadier inspects the interior of a knocked out T-34. The numerous hits confirm that the T-34 menace could be defeated by a combination of steadfast gunnery and steely resolve.

The crew of a tank bivouacking in the field. Any period of rest, however brief, provided a well earned rest from the constant advance.

A Waffen-SS motorcyclist stops to get his bearings, June 1942. Motorcyclists were crucial to the German offensive being more mobile and able to cover large distances much more quickly than other motorised vehicles.

The Waffen-SS made extensive use of the Volkswagen Type 166 *Schwimmwagen* or swimming car. From 1941 to 1944 over 15,000 were made making it the most numerous mass produced amphibious car in history. For crossing the water a screw propeller was lowered down from the rear deck engine cover and a simple coupling connected it to the engine's crankshaft propelling the car forward. To go backwards in the water there was the choice of using a paddle or engaging reverse gear, allowing the turning wheels to slowly rotate the vehicle. The front wheels doubled up as rudders, so steering was done with the wheel on both land and water.

Reconnaissance attached to the Waffen-SS played a vital part in the German advance and later the retreat from Russia, pinpointing enemy positions and searching for cover. Reconnaissance units were responsible for scouting ahead as SS Divisions were often in the vanguard of the fighting in Russia. The grenadier, top, is using a scissors periscope.

Waffen-SS engineers carry out vital repairs to a Sd.Kfz251 halftrack. The fighting, weather and the large distances involved in Russia meant that vehicles were in constant need of servicing or repair.

A Volkswagen *Kubelwagen* and a 10.5cm leFH 18 *leichte FeldHaubitze* or light field howitzer move up to the front. The 10.5cm leFH 18 had a range of over 1,000 metres and a fire rate of 4-6 rounds per minute.

Waffen-SS troops watch the battle from their *Sonderkraftfahrzeug* 251 or Sd.Kfz 251 armoured fighting vehicle built by the Hanomag company. Heavily armoured it was a versatile vehicle which was well liked by the troops and known simply as a *"Hanomag"* by both German and Allied soldiers.

Waffen-SS troops prepare to attack. They were better equipped than the *Wehrmacht* and despite accounting for only a small proportion of the total number of German troops involved in the East, often formed the spearhead of the attack.

A grenadier from the 8th SS Calvary Panzer Division *Florian Geyer* holds an anti-tank "Teller" mine to use against a Russian T-34 tank. Shaped like a plate and packed with 5.5 kilograms of high explosive with a detonation pressure of about 200 pounds, the teller mine was capable of blowing the tracks off any Soviet tank.

The 17cm K 18 in MrsLaf in action by day and night. It had a maximum range of 18 miles and was used to provide long range counter battery support.

A parade of *Das Reich* troops saluting, 1942. The division was decimated following Army Group Centre's failure to take Moscow and was sent to France to rest and regroup.

Waffen-SS troops rescue a badly injured soldier. Waffen-SS Divisions often received a far higher proportion of casualties than other army divisions reflecting their front line role and fanatical attitude.

A Panzer commences the German offensive to capture Stalingrad in the late summer of 1942. By the end of the year the German campaign in the East had come to a halt. The Battle of Stalingrad was the largest battle on the Eastern Front and was a crushing defeat for Germany. It was a turning point in the war and after it the German forces never again had a major strategic victory in the East.

Panzers are massed for a concentrated attack during "Operation Citadel" or the Battle of Kursk.

The Battle of Kursk pitched 900,000 Germans with 2,700 tanks and 2,000 aircraft against some 1.3 million Russians with 3,600 tanks and 2,400 aircraft.

Tiger tanks advance during the Battle of Kursk. Although superior in fire power and armour to the Soviet T-34, the Germans had too few of them.

Half tracks and Panzer III tanks assemble prior to the start of the battle. Initially, the Panzer III was the mainstay of the German forces but was completely outclassed by the Soviet T-34.

Tiger tanks and grenadiers press forward in the River Kuban sector. Developed in 1942, the official German designation for the Tiger was *Panzerkampfwagen* Tiger Ausf. E.

A captured American built tank is salvaged and re-used against the Soviets.

Anti-tank troops in ambush position.

The men of the Waffen-SS soon realised that they had caught a tiger by the tail however there was no option but to soldier on regardless.

Men of the reconnaissance section had to be constantly vigilant in every direction.

A Waffen-SS grenadier shows the fatigue of battle. They earned a fearsome reputation for fighting and consequently were often the first choice of many young recruits over the other military services.

Members of the Waffen-SS discuss tactics with a tank commander and then move into position. Operation Citadel was the largest tank battle in history.

Operation Citadel begins. The German plan was to cut off the Kursk salient by making two pincer attacks at its neck. Infantrymen mark the forward edge of the battle line for the *Luftwaffe*.

A 7.5cm anti-tank gun lurks in an ambush position.

Well camouflaged, the anti-tank gun was a potent weapon against the endless waves of Soviet armour.

There was a constant battle behind the lines to keep supplies moving forward to comrades.

In the opening days of the Battle of Kursk the Waffen-SS made rapid progress penetrating deep into Soviet territory.

The German offensive soon ran into trouble when the Soviets retreated behind defensive lines which had been prepared weeks earlier.

Panzer grenadiers shelter behind a destroyed T-34 tank.

The Soviets retreated behind five defensive positions riddled with tens of thousands of mines before counterattacking.

A command post in a Russian tank trench.

Russian resistance stiffens. SS-units are confronted with elite Soviet troops while Ju-87 Stuka dive bombers try to open a passage through enemy lines.

Waffen-SS Flak gunners alert the Stuka bomber pilots operating over the Kursk battle area of their position to prevent friendly fire. Kursk salient, July 1943.

As the Germans pushed forward the Soviets waited for their chance to counterattack. The faces of these young Waffen-SS infantrymen already show the exhaustion of battle.

As the Germans continued the advance they had no idea that the battle plans to eliminate the Kursk bulge had been leaked to Stalin. Despite mounting losses the Germans continued to push forward..

Within a few days of the attack, the offensive ground to halt after 22 miles. The Soviets who had fallen back on vast minefields, guns and armour then counterattacked with their tanks

Rest periods provided the opportunity to prepare for the next attack.

Waffen-SS troops retreat across a river. The Soviets made full use of the natural features around Kursk to pursue and attack the Germans knowing they were vulnerable crossing water.

Waffen-SS troops take cover in a ditch. Defeat is etched on their faces.

The retreat was slowed by the poor conditions of the Russian roads which even in summer could become impassable after a flash storm.

Waffen-SS soldiers received better rations than *Wehrmacht* troops reflecting their elite status in the eyes of Hitler and Himmler. It often caused resentment among regular troops.

This even extended to real luxuries like champagne. Food was essential to maintain morale.

After defeat at the Battle of Kursk, the Germans were effectively in retreat in the East for the rest of the war. Waffen-SS troops were used to slow the Russian advance and impose the maximum number of casualties on the advancing Soviets. In this way it was hoped that they would sue for peace.

A Waffen-SS Grenadier with a Mauser K98 rifle contemplates the fate of his unit.

As the Germans retreated they found themselves at the mercy of not just the Soviet army but also of the Russian landscape. Some of the most bitter fighting took place in the great swamps and forests of northern Russia and the Baltic States.

Supplying the troops with ammunition became a major logistical challenge in these areas.

During the long retreat Waffen-SS units would often counterattack the advancing Russians, giving the regular army time to withdraw to more strategic lines of defence. However, they only brought temporary relief due to the sheer weight of numbers the Soviets were throwing into the advance.

Waffen-SS troops under fire in the Battle of Narva in 1944. Joined by Estonian volunteers the Waffen-SS fought a very successful rearguard action depriving Stalin of Estonia as a base for air and seaborne attacks against Finland for seven and a half months.

The SS Division *Nord* was is involved in heavy defensive fighting in Finland.

The tanks "skirts" were to protect them against anti-tank rifles and close range anti-tank weapons.

A Waffen-SS machine gunner takes aim.

A forward observer with a scissors periscope.

The attack starts.

Waffen-SS infantry await the next development on the battlefield.

A heavy machine-gun, east of Ripac

No bridge far and wide, so the stream has to be forded.

*SS-Oberscharführer* and commander of tank IV of the 3<sup>rd</sup> SS *Totenkopf* Division.

Artillery and mountian troops of the *Prinz Eugen* Division.

The long march: Kupa - Slunj - Bihac - Vrtoce - Petrovac - Grahovo - Livno - Lise - Mostar - Nevesinje - Gacko - Bileca - Niksic - Gvozd - Savnik.

A four barrelled anti-aircraft gun manned by volunteer soldiers from Boznia and Herzegovina.

*Sturmbannführer* Klingenberg (killed in acton) giving the men light machine-gun training.

General Woehler, Commander-in-Chief of the 8th Army was full of praise for the men of the Waffen-SS: "With an unflinching fighting spirit, they fulfilled all their assignments... Like a rock in the middle of the army whether in defence or in attack."

The battle at Byelgorod - an assault gun successfully tackles an anti-tank ditch.

*SS-Standartenführer* Karl Ullrich distinguished himself in the hard battle at Kursk. He was later the last divisional commander of the 5th Panzer Division *Wiking*.

Panther tanks with infantry riding on top of them, roll into battle.

The Panther was a welcome addition to the fighting strength of the Waffen-SS divisions.

An SS sniper and target spotting observer in a concealed position.

A sniper awaits his target.

Men of the *Florian Geyer* Cavalry Division.

Captured Russian weapons are salvaged and re-used for fighting.

*Panzergrenadiers* of the *Deutschland* Regiment.

Getting ready to attack in the cover of an anti-tank ditch.

The rifle grenade is fired from a cup attached to the barrel and has a great fragmentation effect.

Waffen-SS grenadiers advance tentatively into combat.

The Tiger tank was far superior to the Soviet T-34, but there simply wasn't enough of them. By the end of the war the Germans had produced nearly 6,000 Panthers and just over 1,300 Tiger tanks. In comparison the Russians were building over 1,200 T-34 tanks a month.

A PaK 40 75mm anti-tank gun – the backbone of German anti-tank guns in the final years of the war.

Anti-tank guns and self-propelled field guns protect the flanks during the break-out.

The Waffen-SS were forced to endure four merciless winters on the Eastern Front.

Waffen-SS grenadiers watch the German retreat. Despite morale plummeting in the *Heer*, the Waffen-SS maintained a fanatical fighting spirit to the end.

The third winter of fighting in Russia was particularly hard as the Germans were in full retreat. Hitler's orders to "stand fast and fight to the death" resulted in the needless death of many Waffen-SS troops.

Tiger tanks retreat through the Russian winter in December 1943. Its formidable 88mm gun was feared by the Soviets, but it was over engineered and consequently proved difficult to repair.

A German soldier up to his waist in snow makes slow progress with his MG 42 machine gun. The weather compounded the misery.

The break-outs from the Kowel and Korsun-Cherkassy or Tscherkassy pockets against overwhelming Soviet odds sealed the fanatical fighting spirit of the Waffen-SS *Wiking* Division.

The photographer was attracted by the contrast between the vehicles as one overtakes the other.

Tank men and grenadiers are dependent on each other.

Panther tanks of the *Wiking* tank regiment played a decisive part in the successful break out from the Korsun-Tscherkassy Pocket. It easily outclassed any Soviet tank and was meant to replace the Panzer III and IVs which were susceptible to the Soviet T-34 but was never available in sufficient numbers.

A break between operations. On the left: The commander of a Panther tank unit reports to *Gruppenführer* or Lieutenant Colonel Gille. On the right: The commander of the tank regiment: Johannes-Rudolf Mühlenkamp.

*SS-Obersturmführer* or Lieutenant Colonel Erwin Meier-Dress, Knights Cross, August 1944. A Panzer Ace, he was killed a year later trying to relieve the Soviet siege of Budapest.

The cost in lives of defending the constantly moving German line against the vast numerical superiority of the Russian forces always fell disproportionately on infantrymen.

Panther tanks of the SS Division *Wiking* fighting east of Warsaw.

Waffen-SS troops are sent in to put down the Warsaw uprising, August 1944. They did, but with characteristic ruthlessness.

Exhausted Waffen-SS troops push supplies up to the front in an improvised cart attached to a bicycle. Controversially the Soviets stopped short of the city allowing the Germans to put down the uprising. The Poles held out for 63 days with little outside support.

German troops rest during the uprising. 16,000 Poles died, German casualties were about 8,000. But the real victims were the civilians of Warsaw. Between 150,000 and 200,000 of them died, mostly from the fighting and mass murder.

Initially the Poles took over the city centre but in savage house to house fighting the Germans took back control in September 1944. In all, 25% of Warsaw buildings were destroyed and together with earlier damage over 85% of the city had been razed to the ground when the Soviets finally entered in January 1945.

Waffen-SS troops under fire. Feared and loathed by the Soviets in equal measure, if they were captured they were often executed on sight.

The Russians enter a village in Poland as Waffen-SS troops seek to counterattack. Even this defensive action could not make up for the Soviets overwhelming superiority in men and material.

A shell explodes just in front of a unit of Waffen-SS troops. During the long retreat in the East they were used strategically, often to relieve encircled *Wehrmacht* divisions.

Officers of the 5<sup>th</sup> Company of the *Wiking* Panzer Regiment pictured on the engine deck of a Panther tank, Russia, Summer 1944.

Destroyed Soviet T-34 tanks litter a battlefield as Waffen-SS troops look on. With over 20 million dead, both civilian and military, the Russians paid a huge price in liberating their homeland and fighting their way to the centre of Berlin.

Waffen-SS troops rest in a hastily made trench. The Soviet advance was so quick that it proved difficult to prepare proper defensive lines.

A Waffen-SS sniper in action. Snipers worked in twos, one to look for targets and the other to take the shot.

Waffen-SS troops fire an 8cm Granatwerfer 34 mortar. It was the standard German mortar used throughout the war and had a reputation for extreme accuracy and a rapid rate of fire.

A Waffen-SS radio station command post. Unlike the start of the war German lines of communication often broke down completely during the long retreat in the East.

Tank men and infantrymen on the Eastern Front.

Waffen-SS troops hitch a ride on the back of a Panzer tank. From 1944 onwards they found themselves in almost constant retreat.

Waffen-SS troops shelter behind a knocked out T-34 tank.

The Germans also developed new weapons. Here we see infantrymen with an assault StG 44 carabine rifle. It could fire 500-600 rounds a minute and had an effective range of 800 metres.

An anti-tank *Jadgpanzer* 38t or "Hetzer" gun belonging to the *Florian Geyer* Division is brought up to the front. A light anti-tank gun, it was massed produced but suffered from having thin armour.

Due to intensive Waffen-SS resistance Hungary was not to fall to the Soviets until the spring of 1945.

*Obertsturmbannführer* Leon Degrelle during the retreat of his division to the border of the *Reich*. Commander of the 28th Waffen-SS Division *Walloon* from Belgium, he was severely wounded in 1944 and was one of only three foreigners to win the Oak Leaves to the Knights Cross.

In the high mountains of Yugoslavia the Waffen-SS fought an intensive battle with Josip Broz Tito's partisans throughout 1944 and up to May 1945. They were a communist lead resistance movement that in 1944 numbered over 800,000 men in 52 divisions. Waffen-SS troops are seen here with a captured French tank.

The Waffen-SS took heavy casualties in 1944 and 1945 along the whole of the Eastern Front. Many of the later divisions were only regimental or brigade sized units who lacked the fighting spirit of the earlier ones.

A reconnaissance troop makes its way to the Russian line in the northern sector of the Eastern front. Unlike the *Wehrmacht*, morale amongst the Waffen-SS generally remained high.

Waffen-SS troops try in vain to stem the Soviet advance. Here, infantrymen from the regiment *Der Führer* await the oncoming Soviet forces.

By 1944 severe shortages of winter clothing meant that they had to rely on the generosity of civilians who were asked by the Nazi regime to donate furs and other winter coats.

German troops rest behind "snow walls" in the winter of 1944 on the Eastern front. Given the speed of the Russian offensive they were often the only defensive positions they could construct.

A Hummel or "bumble-bee" self propelled artillery gun arrives at the front. It had a 15cm howitzer and was first used in the Battle of Kursk. It had an operational range of over 130 miles. By the end of the war over 700 had been built.

In the East the Waffen-SS found themselves having to defend an ever collapsing German front in which the line was regularly overrun by Soviets troops.

Shortage of heavy armour and tanks in the last 6 months of the war saw Waffen-SS troops trying to stop Russian tanks with machine guns.

An SS Cavalry Division officer discusses the worsening situation in the East with his troops. To the end Waffen-SS troops carried out localised counter-thrusts against the Soviet juggernaut. Meant to bring relief for a few crucial days, they often ended in the death of most of those taking part.

In the closing year of the war ammunition was rationed as supply lines to the German front in the East collapsed.

As the Soviets advanced through Poland in late 1944, the German administration collapsed. Over 600,000 Soviet soldiers died fighting German troops in Poland. A Communist-controlled adminstration, headed by Bolesław Bierut, was installed by the Soviets in July in Lublin, the first major Polish city to be seized by Russia from Germany.

Waffen-SS tanks from the 3rd Division *Totenkopf* and snipers in Poland, July 1944. After the Soviets launched Operation Bagration, the largest and last offensive to be launched from Russian soil, the SS Panzer Corps were the only line of defence after the destruction of Army Group Centre.

Waffen-SS troops man an 88mm anti-aircraft gun and retreat across a bridge in a halftrack while a knocked out German tank lies in the river. By February 1945 the whole of Poland was under Soviet control.

A Waffen-SS soldier loads a 30mm *Schießbecher* or "shooting cup" grenade onto his K98 rifle. It was effective against infantry, fortifications and light armoured vehicles up to a range of 280 metres.

As the Germans retreated they employed a scorched earth policy to deprive the Red Army of anything of value. However, the sheer speed of the Soviet advance often caught the Germans off guard.

A Waffen-SS soldier uses his body as an improvised stand while another soldier fires the MG 42 machine gun. By 1945 much of the Waffen-SS armour had been destroyed.

The Waffen-SS in Hungary fought a more successful rearguard action, holding out until 1945. By the end of the war over 300,000 Hungarian soldiers and 80,000 civilians had died.

Waffen-SS units fought furiously in the Baltic in defence of East Prussia but the Soviets still marched into the region in January 1945, the first German state to be occupied in the East.

A lack of heavy weapons meant infantrymen had to fight the Russians with "*Haftladungen*" or hand held mines.

When the Red Army crossed the border of the *Reich*, panic set in. A quickly dug defensive position on the outskirts of a town in Lower-Silesia.

As the Soviets fought their way to Berlin, German defences collapsed, although some towns continued to hold out, often at huge cost to both soldiers and civilians.

Demoralised, defeated and exhausted, Waffen-SS troops contemplate their fate at the hands of the Soviets.

A Waffen-SS soldier emerges from a trench. Many of the thirty-eight Waffen-SS divisions were decimated by the end of the war.

As the Soviets advanced through Germany, Waffen-SS resistance intensified but with a huge numerical supremacy in men and material the final outcome was never in doubt.

Units of the Waffen-SS defend the town of Küstrin. The unexpected arrival of Soviet troops at the end of January 1945 at the ancient fortress and garrison town came as a tremendous shock to the German High Command – the Soviets were now only 50 miles from Berlin itself. Two Soviet armies lay siege to the town. Despite this the Germans held out for 60 days but at an appalling human cost – about 5,000 Germans were killed, 9,000 wounded and 6,000 captured. The Russians lost 5,000 killed and 15,000 wounded.

The Battle of Berlin was the last major offensive battle in the East. Intensive street battles left much of the city in ruins. In the defence of Berlin over 100,000 German soldiers were killed before Hitler committed suicide on 30 April 1945. Over 125,000 civilians also died in the battle.

After hostilities had finally ceased on 8 May 1945 nearly one in three Waffen-SS troops were dead or missing in action. To put their mortality rate in context it was the equivalent of all the casualties suffered by the United States military during the entire war.